Chakras

A Chakra-based Meditation For Abundant Life: A Balanced Manifestation

(How To Open And Balance Your Chakras For Beginners)

Lauren Andrade

TABLE OF CONTENT

The Human Body's Chakras 1

Seven Important Chakras 21

Internal Awakening To The Universe 54

The Microcosm Internally 61

Your Sacral Chakra May Be Blocked. 66

Visualization And Meditation 92

Yellow 103

Methods For Opening Your Third Eye 108

Dream Journaling 124

Advice For Harmonizing Your Sacral Chakra 140

The Electrical Aspects Of Rrofound Discovery 150

The Human Body's Chakras

Now that we have a better understanding of the chakras, we can examine what each one represents. There are seven major chakras, and when they are all functioning properly and releasing the correct amount of energy, you will feel incredible. You will be able to handle whatever comes your way, feel energized, and have no pain, negative thoughts, or other problems. Nonetheless, when the chakras are closed off or overly open (both of which can cause problems), some aspect of your existence will suffer. These chakra points will influence various aspects of your existence, including your psychic abilities, emotions, and physical health, and they include:

planetary star chakra

The earth star chakras are significant because they are responsible for connecting you to the earth's elemental energies. You will feel more grounded and be able to think more logically as a result of this. Despite the fact that you must acknowledge yourself as a Being of Light when working with the chakras, there are times when you must be grounded in reality to avoid having misguided emotions and thoughts. You should also find a means to be grounded so that you can participate in the present moment and remember your life's highest purpose.

When the earth star chakra is not sufficiently open, logical thought becomes difficult. You may constantly have your mind in the clouds, and conversing with others about the decisions you must make may seem tedious. This indicates that you need to incorporate additional grounding in order to feel better and focus on your daily activities. On the other hand, when the star chakra is overly open, you may experience problems such as overthinking or feeling too grounded and anxious about current events.

This chakra will be located below your ankles. This chakra is associated with the colors maroon, black, and silver. Garnet, tiger's eye, hematite, and onyx are all crystals and gemstones that will assist you in healing the earth stone chakra.

The main center

Root chakra is the subsequent chakra. This is the source of your functional physical energy and is responsible for anchoring it within your physical being. This region will be responsible for relationships, particularly how they relate to you within the group, survival concerns, and family. It is considered the foundation chakra because it is responsible for all of your corporeal qualities and aspects. The root chakra is located at the base of the vertebrae, on the spiral that leads directly to the earth star chakra. The root chakra is represented by the color red and its element is earth. It even has its own note, the G immediately below middle C.

When your root chakra is healthy, your senses of scent and touch will be healthy, and your sense of smell can function as a psychic ability. This means that you may be able to sense and smell unseen entities, which those with a weak root chakra cannot comprehend.

If you wish to supplement the energies emanating from the root chakra, it is recommended that you wear healing and motivational gemstones, such as red quartz, red jasper, garnet, tourmaline, bloodstone, or ruby. When the root chakra is functioning properly, it is responsible for healing the circulatory and skeletal systems, your hips, skin, feet, legs, and kidneys, among other things, and when it is used correctly, it helps you understand how the world is interconnected by allowing you to be more grounded and even stronger when confronting uncertain situations.

Sacral center

The sacral chakra is located in the lower abdomen and aids in your ability to communicate with others and engage in exciting experiences. It is also associated with sexuality, prosperity, health, and a sense of delight. This is a highly emotional chakra because it governs your ability to form relationships with others. It is associated with your sexual energy and your creativity, and it enables you to search within to interpret what others are saying.

You can locate the sacral chakra by peering a few inches below the navel. This chakra is associated with the color orange, so amber, carnelian, and coral gemstones are ideal. If you are experiencing issues with your large intestine, bladder, kidneys, lymphatic system, reproductive organs, or lower back, the sacral chakra is the one you should focus on.

The sacral chakra

The solar plexus chakra is located near the upper abdomen, and it is the one that demonstrates your ability to be self-assured and in charge of your life, while also coping with any self-worth and self-esteem issues that may arise. If this chakra has issues, you may experience diminished self-esteem, a bad day, or other negative feelings about yourself.

Those who experience a great deal of diminished self-esteem may have a solar plexus that is not functioning optimally. This chakra will help you feel like you have a superior sense of self, and it will strengthen your sense of integrity and honor, as well as your ability to empower others. This one is related to your mental energy because it will give you the ability to make sound decisions, and it is often related to your intuition. It will ensure that you are also capable of managing these emotional energies.

The solar plexus is located directly below the sternum and approximately two inches above the navel. The color associated with the solar plexus chakra is yellow, and the corresponding element in nature is fire. If you have a healthy and active solar plexus chakra, it indicates that your intuition are often accurate and active, and that you have a good sense of sight. The most effective gemstones for the solar plexus chakra are amber, tiger's eyes, gold topaz, and numerous crystals with a gold or yellow hue.

If you are experiencing an issue with your digestive system, activating the solar plexus chakra will be beneficial, particularly for your pancreas, gallbladder, stomach, small intestine, and liver. When this chakra is in balance, it will help you feel courageous, generous, self-disciplined, and gives you a great deal of confidence and excellent ethics. It essentially turns you into a warrior. But if it is not working well, you will feel like you have no personal identity, that you give too much to others when it is not necessary, and that your self-esteem is stuck at rock bottom.

Chakra centrale

As you might infer from the name, the heart chakras relate to your capacity to love those around you. This chakra is located in the center of the thorax, directly above the heart. Not only does it aid in love, but also in healing, serenity, and happiness. This chakra is concerned with compassion, forgiveness, and affection. Whatever emotional anguish you are experiencing will transform you based on your circumstances. Due to its location in the center of the body, this chakra concentrates on love as its own source of life. This chakra will be associated with the colors green and pink, and when it is functioning appropriately, your sense of touch will become more sensitive.

In addition to assisting with affection and compassion for others, the heart chakra is excellent for assisting with all aspects of the respiratory system. This includes the components of the diaphragm, heart, and lungs. As the name implies, this mantra asserts that love is always the greatest force. Love is the most essential thing, and it is a form of respect and care that you can give to others and to yourself.

When the heart chakra is functioning properly, you will experience feelings of hope, compassion, devotion, serenity, and even kindness toward others. When the heart chakra is neglected, however, it is simpler to experience feelings of jealousy and anger. Often, resentment rises to the surface, making it difficult to absolve others. You can isolate yourself from others and even become somewhat furtive as a result. Therefore, it is crucial to give your heart chakra the attention it requires so that you can only experience positive emotions.

Throat chakra

This chakra will assist you in entering the realm of unconditional affection. This person can assist you in receiving healing, wisdom, and divine illumination. When this chakra is functioning, everything in your life will become clearer, and you will be more receptive to what others have to say. You embrace others for who they are rather than attempting to change them. This is a very essential chakra because it is regarded as the gateway to the highest life path and is the source of all intent. For instance, whenever you are angry, the thymus chakra will attempt to prevent you from uttering something that you will later regret.

Between the heart and throat chakras, you will locate the thymus chakra. This one will be associated with the colors purple, green, and aqua, as it is your energy source. Additionally, you will find that many people associate this with the endocrine system, the immune system, and the thymus gland. The white fire will be the symbol for this one.

There are numerous psychic abilities associated with this chakra. When it is in excellent working order, you can have lucid dreams and the ability to be completely receptive to others. It is simpler for you to express your emotions to others as well as your affection for those you care about. However, when the thymus chakra is blocked, you lack inner strength and are more easily manipulated by others. You will deny the assistance of others as well as your own spirituality. You become withdrawn and may have difficulty expressing your emotions, and you will either judge others hastily or believe that they are judging you.

thymus chakra

Following the heart chakra is the pharynx chakra. This is the one that allows you to effectively express yourself and communicate your desired messages. You can use this chakra to be more creative, and you will have sufficient willpower and options to make healthful decisions. You will strive to uphold your personal integrity and honor all of your commitments to others. The throat chakra facilitates the connection between the heart and the intellect, and its location in the throat signifies your ability to communicate. It is often associated with telling the truth and being able to express oneself effectively.

If you discover that your throat chakra is damaged, you are likely dealing with a great deal of suppressed emotions. Frequently, these emotions will go unnoticed, but if you don't give them the attention they require, they can negatively impact your entire day.

The color sky blue is associated with the pharynx chakra. This chakra focuses on revealing your soul's truth and imparting the necessary wisdom. As the throat chakra is responsible for communication, it is the one that enables you to express yourself. It is located at the base of the throat and will assist you in exercising your own fortitude as the nourishment your soul requires.

The brow region

This chakra is the one that will enable you to focus on your surroundings and see the big picture. This one is located directly between the eyes on the forehead and is often associated with intuition, sagacity, and cognitive ability. This will serve as the epicenter of your intuition, intellect, and visions. If you have the ability to communicate with and see spirits, you can credit your third eye. Because you have refined your psychic abilities, you are going to be more sensitive to motion, sounds, and other things that others may not notice.

This chakra will enable you to discover and evaluate your own insights. It will use the knowledge you have gained from life experience to assist you in making decisions. If you are able to allow this third eye to function, you demonstrate faith in a higher power and it becomes simpler to align yourself with unseen forces.

The third eye chakra is located exactly in the center of the forehead, between the eyebrows. This chakra will be composed of either an indigo blue or a violet hue. If this chakra is functioning properly, you will be endowed with innate knowledge and enjoy the benefit of knowing yourself thoroughly. You may possess additional abilities, such as clairvoyance and telepathy. Due to its location, the third eye chakra works well with numerous systems, including the entire nervous system, brain, and cranium, as well as your sense organs, pituitary gland, skull, and eyes.

When this chakra is not functioning properly, you may feel disinterested in some of the things you ordinarily enjoy doing or bored. You can become excessively judgmental and unduly critical of others. You will overthink the events occurring in your life and frequently lack the creativity required to complete tasks. Activating the third eye chakra can aid in resolving these issues and provide you with the requisite insight for all of your decisions.

Throat Chakra

This one will be located at the very top of the head, and it is frequently associated with your spirituality as well as your outer and inner attractiveness. The summit chakra will be the point of connection between your spiritual consciousness and your Higher Self. It connects you to higher dimensions so that you can attain a higher level of enlightenment. This is one of the most significant chakras because it is located at the top of the body, where it is easiest for other worlds to communicate.

This one will be purple, white, or gold due to its proximity to your head's crown. When this chakra is activated, your spiritual awareness will be awoken and you will become more attuned with the universe as a whole. Instead of focusing on all the emotional burden that has kept you in the past, you will begin to live in the present. You also understand when to let go.

As you can see, the chakras influence various areas of the body and are interconnected. When a chakra is obstructed and not functioning properly, it begins to influence your life and the various aspects associated with that chakra. However, if ignored for an extended period of time, this condition can worsen and begin to affect other chakras as well. Therefore, it is essential to learn about your chakras and how to take care of them properly.

Seven Important Chakras

The Root Chakra is the first Chakra.

Where: at the perineum at the base of the spine

Your root chakra is appropriately named, as it is the chakra nearest to the earth. Activating the root chakra allows you to become grounded. Moreover, this chakra is the one that controls your inclinations for survival.

This chakra's equilibrium is what allows you to become impassioned, energetic, creative, and courageous.

Your adrenal glands and large intestines are associated with the first chakra. Additionally, it is connected to the skeletal system. It controls your response to combat or flight. Therefore, you must sustain your Root chakra for these systems to function optimally. The associated body segment with this chakra is the lower extremities.

A properly activated and balanced root chakra produces a feeling of safety. It also helps you become more aware of your surroundings while simultaneously allowing your thoughts, emotions, and actions to remain unaffected by them.

A blockage in the first chakra, on the other hand, causes insecurity. You experience nervousness and social anxiety, and you fear that people will not embrace you. Consequently, you exhibit defensive behaviors. In addition to causing you to lose motivation, a blocked Root chakra also leads to procrastination.

But when the Root chakra is overactive as a result of overcompensating for other obstructed chakras, you have a tendency to become materialistic and greedy.

The Sacral Chakra is the second chakra.

Where: in the lower abdomen, between the spine's base and the navel

The second chakra houses your erotic feelings. It is the location of your desire for physical delight, sex, and procreation. This chakra is responsible for your feelings of contentment and open-mindedness. Simply stated, it allows you to enjoy life and all its infinite possibilities.

The organs associated with the sacral chakra are the kidneys and bladder. In addition, homeostasis in this chakra is essential for the proper operation of your circulatory and reproductive systems.

When the Sacral chakra is activated and in balance, creativity and passion flow freely. It also enables you to express yourself while maintaining emotional control. A balanced sacral chakra alleviates intimacy issues.

In contrast, blockage of the second chakra has the opposite effect. You develop emotional apathy. The experience or thought of pleasure and intercourse induces feelings of guilt.

Conversely, an overactive sacral chakra puts you at risk for being overly emotional. You become excessively sensual and disrespectful of your body.

The Third (Solar Plexus) Chakra

Where: just beneath your sternum and a few inches above your belly button

The third chakra houses emotions such as elation and rage. This is also where your ambitions, determination, and self-esteem reside. Obviously, this chakra plays a significant role in your ability to attain your objectives. Also located in the Solar Plexus chakra is your capacity for empathy.

The organs associated with the third chakra are the digestive system organs. In addition, it is connected to your muscular system and adrenal glands.

A well-balanced and activated third chakra produces assertiveness and self-respect.

In the meantime, an inert third chakra renders you inactive as well. You become slothful, hesitant, and prone to frustration. Individuals whose Solar Plexus chakras are blocked become trapped in the victim role.

A highly active Solar Plexus chakra, on the other hand, has the opposite but still negative effect. You become authoritative and aggressive.

The Fourth Chakra (heart) is the center of the heart.

Where: within the middle of the ribcage

The fourth chakra is associated with your capacity for compassion and unconditional affection. It is the throne of serenity and your soul's abode. When one falls in love, the energy in the heart chakra increases. The energy then descends to your third chakra, where your emotions reside. The energy then descends to the sacral chakra, where your sexual emotions are deposited. There, it will desire for sexual intimacy as a means of release. When this energy is present in the first chakra, you will experience a desire to settle down.

The organs associated with the fourth chakra are the heart and lungs. It is also connected to the thymus gland. In addition, the heart chakra affects the functioning of your limbs and hands.

A properly activated and balanced fourth chakra enables you to be sociable and compassionate toward others. It enables the development and maintenance of healthy, joyful, and loving relationships.

However, when this chakra is deficient, you become frigid and unfeeling. The issue will manifest physically as cardiac maladies and a weakened immune system.

The Fifth (Throat) Chakra

Where: above your shoulder

The fifth chakra is the communication chakra. It governs your ability to express yourself through speech and other mediums, including writing, painting, music, etc. This chakra relates to personal integrity. It enables you to form sensible judgments by allowing you to be aware of what is occurring within and without. Moreover, the fifth chakra is where healing and transformation occur.

The fifth chakra is associated with the thyroid and parathyroid glands. Shoulder and neck are the associated body regions with this chakra.

You become fluent in your discourse as well as other forms of self-expression when your fifth chakra is active and in balance.

The manifestation of a blockage in the fifth chakra is difficulty articulating oneself verbally or otherwise. When this chakra is closed, you may find it challenging to speak the truth.

A hyperactive fifth chakra, on the other hand, will make you a boisterous speaker but a poor listener. You have a tendency to dominate conversations, which repels others and hinders your ability to establish healthy social and intimate relationships.

The sixth (Third Eye) Chakra.

Where: above the center of your eyebrows, in the middle of your forehead

This chakra is also known as the prefrontal chakra. The third eye chakra is where wisdom resides. It also serves as a source of inspiration. It is the location of your intuition. Everyone is capable of clairvoyance, despite popular belief. The third eye chakras of some individuals are activated while those of others are not. Your sixth charka is the focal point of your desires. In this location, your past-life memories reside.

When the brow chakra is activated and in a state of equilibrium, one becomes intuitive and imaginative.

However, when the third eye chakra is blocked, inadequate foresight results. You develop a selective memory. In addition, an inactive sixth chakra increases your risk of developing depression. You also become dependent on others to make choices for you. Similarly, inactive brow chakras result in a sheepish mentality.

On the other hand, if your sixth chakra is overactive, you risk losing contact with reality. You develop unreasonable expectations of the world, resulting in extreme disappointment and a lack of coping skills.

The Crown Chakra (Seventh Chakra)

Where: on top of one's cranium

The seventh chakra is responsible for information management. Nonetheless, it is more than that. The crown chakra is your connection to higher energies. It represents your relationship with the divine. It has a connection to transcendence and universality. It is where you will discover your spiritual will and authentic self.

The crown chakra rules over the central nervous system and cerebral cortex.

A properly activated and balanced seventh chakra enables you to attain the highest level of self-awareness.

However, if the seventh chakra is blocked, you may experience moderate to severe psychological impairments. It also hinders your ability to cultivate spiritual awareness.

On the other hand, hyperactive seventh chakras result in either unduly cerebral thought or spiritual obsession.

The fourth chakra, the heart chakra

The heart chakra is also known as Anahata, which means unbeaten or a sound produced without striking.

Also referred to as the heart center or 'that which is even new'

This chakra is represented by a green lotus flower with 12 petals and two intersecting triangles within a green circle.

The associated gland is the thymus, and the organ is the epidermis, the body's largest organ.

It is located in the center of the thorax in the region of the heart, and its colors are pink and green. Pink is associated with psychological health, whereas green is a very calming, harmonizing color.

Diet plays a significant role in our health and wellbeing. In the end, you truly are what you consume.

The heart chakra is associated with the consumption of vegetables, particularly greens. Choose verdant greens such as spinach, kale, and salad greens in addition to Brussels sprouts, peas, and asparagus. You may also select green fruits like green grapes, avocados, and kiwis. Additionally, it includes green superfoods such as green tea, spirulina, and wheatgrass.

Green, pink, or a combination of the two can be used to balance the energy of the heart chakra when working with therapeutic crystals. When selecting green crystals, aventurine, malachite, jade, peridot, and emerald are all viable options. You can choose between rose quartz, kunzite, morganite, rhodonite, and rhodochrosite if you wish to deal with pink crystals. You may also choose to work with unakite, which has a very balancing energy for the heart chakra and is a combination of green and pink.

Bergamot, rose, neroli, lavender, geranium, and sandlewood have an affinity for the heart chakra if you enjoy working with aromatherapy oils and massage.

The vitality emanating from the heart chakra.

This is the central chakra of the entire chakra system, the system's center.

Clearly, the heart chakra affects matters of the heart, including relationships, affection, and compassion. Additionally, it influences spirituality and self-acceptance.

It has physical effects on the heart, blood pressure, lungs and respiratory system, upper back, and limbs.

The modern Western lifestyle appears to wreak havoc on the heart chakra. Heart disease is a serious issue, a leading cause of death, and millions of people suffer from heart disease, high blood pressure, poor circulation, and respiratory problems, all of which are debilitating conditions that limit one's ability to live life to the fullest.

The heart is a biological mechanism whose function is to circulate oxygen-rich blood throughout the body. It transports all necessary substances to all body parts and then eliminates all contaminants through the kidneys, liver, and lungs. When viewed in this light, it becomes clear how important a healthy heart is to our entire system.

However, in our pursuit of success, instant gratification, exhilaration, and material wealth, we have lost the ability to appreciate the things that truly matter. We often refer to those who follow their heart rather than their mind as dreamers, but this is meant as an insult. However, some of our most brilliant minds have been visionaries.

Albert Einstein said

"Imagination has greater value than knowledge. For knowledge is limited to what we currently know and understand, whereas imagination encompasses the entire world and everything that will ever be known and understood."

Even the medical community is beginning to recognize the connection between our mental and emotional health and physical health. High blood pressure and heart disease are often physical manifestations of stress, chronic anger or frustration, and the repression of significant emotional suffering.

Every life will contain disappointments, losses, problems, and challenges; however, when the heart chakra is balanced, all of these events can be processed with positive energy, granting you a sense of equilibrium and acceptance, as well as the ability to see beyond the immediate problems.

The heart chakra serves as the chakra system's focal point, harmonizing the lower physical chakras with the higher spiritual chakras. When it is in equilibrium, it allows you to establish equilibrium throughout your complete system.

Creating a life/work balance, creating balance in relationships, rather than being overly demanding or self-pitying, creating balance between physical and emotional requirements, enabling you to see opportunities for growth and development, and balancing the material and spiritual aspects of your life.

A blocked heart chakra can result in paranoia, fear of betrayal, indecisiveness, shyness, resentment, and jealously.

A blocked heart chakra can make it difficult for a person to experience genuine love, causing them to engage in a series of short, intense relationships, in which they seek love but only find pain and emotional instability.

This can be observed in both platonic and romantic relationships, as a constant series of betrayals, disappointments, and abandonments. This can lead to a downward trajectory in which you become unable to trust and believe in yourself, and begin to wonder, 'Why can't I find love? What is the matter with me?'

The fear of being betrayed can cause you to shun intimacy altogether, choosing to disregard the emotion out of fear of betrayal, and possessiveness or jealousy will destroy any chance of genuine happiness.

A balanced heart chakra enables you to love yourself, which is the first step in being able to love others. You will be able to appreciate your own emotions and then those of others.

It will bring a sense of internal balance that will enhance your self-confidence and self-esteem, allowing you to have a healthy connection with others and build successful relationships founded on mutual respect, trust, and compassion.

Achieving a balance between the material and spiritual aspects of our world is essential for pleasure and health.

A balanced heart chakra and the ability to follow your emotions are not obstacles to success; on the contrary, they lead to greater self- and social-awareness.

You have a strong sense of safety and security, which enables you to be open, compassionate, and forgiving, as well as to emanate positive energy.

Time is not wasted on pleasure, creativity, enjoyment, and affection; these are the things that make life worthwhile. When you prioritize them, everything else will fall into order.

The heart chakra has an effect.

The heart chakra is therefore physically, emotionally, and spiritually associated with the heart.

Heart chakra energy is associated with compassion, affection, and spirituality. It involves the capacity to maintain wholesome relationships with others and with oneself.

Physically, it can affect the cardiovascular system, respiratory system, and immune system.

It is the area of your energy system associated with self-assurance, self-respect, self-expression, originality, generosity, compassion, and respect.

This chakra enables us to recognize the significance of living with compassion and benevolence for ourselves and others.

The heart chakra resonates with the force of universal affection for all beings.

In Balance.

When it is in equilibrium, you have a sense of internal equilibrium and a healthy connection to others and to your relationships. The balance between material and spiritual requirements is possible. You are compassionate and capable of unconditionally giving affection. You are also capable of nurturing yourself and others.

Lacking balance.

When the heart chakra is out of balance, you may experience indecision, paranoia, a fear of betrayal, or a general sense of self-pity. It can manifest as timidity, isolation, resentment, or an excessive possessiveness or jealousy.

Additionally, it can manifest as a dread of solitude and a fear of commitment. A tendency to demand attention, which is sometimes perceived as the martyr or pitiful me syndrome.

In this chakra, ancient traumas are also stored. This chakra can be affected by past hurts, losses, or anxieties, leading to an inability to set healthy boundaries.

This loneliness, grief, or depression can result in physical deterioration, general illness, and an impaired immune system.

Physically, it can cause heart disease, tension, asthma, high blood pressure, circulatory issues, breast issues, lung disease, respiratory difficulties, and cancers. Additionally, it can encompass issues with the arms, hands, and fingers.

The Third Eye: The Source of Extraordinary Abilities

Humankind has believed in the concept of the third eye for thousands of years. Almost everywhere can be found depictions of the third eye and the pinecone, which is a symbol of the pineal gland. Egyptians believed in this notion.

Hindus and Buddhists continue to hold a firm belief in the third vision.

We held the third eye in such high regard because we knew it could unleash a number of extraordinary abilities. In addition to knowledge, intelligence, and wisdom, the third eye can activate psychic abilities. When your third eye is aroused, your vision of the world improves. You possess an all-seeing eye that allows you to witness things that others cannot.

This is why most individuals who are intrigued by the occult and extraordinary phenomena are captivated by the concept of the third eye.

If your third eye is aroused, you may possess some of these abilities.

Clairvoyance (Psychic Visions)

It is the power of clairvoyant vision. This indicates that you can see things that others cannot. This talent has always been regarded as a boon. Nonetheless, we all possess this capacity to some extent. Some young children have more developed clairvoyance than adults. They can perceive spirits, energies, and impending misfortunes. Their minds are not completely developed enough to comprehend the meanings of certain signals, but they see more clearly. As we age, the pineal gland calcifies, diminishing our psychic abilities.

Pineal gland decalcification is also involved in the activation of the third sight. It aids in enhancing our perceptual abilities. We are more sensitive to the presence of energies, spirits, and portents. We may be able to deduce the precise meanings of those signals as our minds develop.

This is one of the most sought-after intuitive abilities, as it gives you a firm grasp on events around you. Even events that have not yet occurred can be predicted with some degree of accuracy.

This is not the result of sorcery. Your mind is capable of perceiving energies. Your body is an intensely energetic sphere. You can perceive these energies when your third eye is awakened and your perception increases. This heightened perception sets you apart from other individuals. You begin to see things without the deductions or judgments of our biases. Your vision and experiences become more distinct.

Once your third eye has been opened, you can develop clairvoyant abilities through meditation.

Examining Auras

This entire universe consists of energy. As part of the universe, we too are energy. Energy's unique characteristic is that it emanates itself. Every living thing has an electromagnetic energy field that encompasses the entire organism. This energy field is known as the aura. Our organism is more than merely a physical form. Emotional, etheric, mental, astral, and celestial energies exist within the body as well. All of these energies emanate color-based radiations or auras. These colors are visible and can be used to determine the type of energy that dominates a person. This practice is known as aura observation.

When your third eye becomes active and fully functional, you can develop the ability to see auras and energy fields. The majority of us possess this power, but it is rarely very potent. Yet, when you visit a place or encounter a person, you can sense the presence of negative energy or vibe. You do not need others to inform you of this. The awakening of the third eye merely multiplies this ability several times. You will have the ability to discern auras without opening your eyes. You will be able to perceive auras that have no corporeal bodies. You will see energy, darkness, and light in their most vivid manifestation.

This ability begins to develop naturally when you meditate and activate your third eye. Negative or positive energies will be perceptible to you. The vibes emanating from people will be very distinct and strong, and you won't need an introduction to determine a person's fundamental characteristics. If you wish to develop this skill, meditation and concentration are the primary means to do so.

Astral Travel or Astral Projection

Astral Projection is a method for experiencing out-of-body sensations. Again, this is a skill that we all possess to some extent. During near-death experiences, traumas, and ailments, individuals may feel as if they have left their bodies and traveled a great distance. However, such circumstances are never voluntarily chosen.

Astral travel is more accurately characterized as "dreaming while awake." We are made up of energies. You can cause your energies to exit your body and travel at will, thanks to the third eye's psychic abilities. As in other dimensions, astral travel is limited in duration, but the duration of your experience can be extraordinarily lengthy. You can communicate with other energies that lack a physical form. You are able to travel far and return. You retain total control over yourself. You will be able to perceive the world from an entirely new angle. Your perspective on the world would shift drastically.

Despite the projection's mystical appearance, it is an actuality. We are not simply this organism. This body is a negligible portion of our genuine being. When this organism ceases to function, we will not merely perish. According to the energy levels, we will continue to live eternally. You can develop astral projection abilities by routinely awakening and strengthening your third eye through meditation.

All of these abilities are real, but they are dormant because we do not routinely exercise them. By routinely practicing them, you can make them more robust.

It is essential, however, that you thoroughly develop your powers before beginning to use these abilities. Not all surrounding energies are positive and innocuous. There are many negative energies in the universe, and they will attempt to interact with or influence you. If you lack adequate protection, you may succumb to their influence and cause yourself injury.

Meditation is one of the most effective methods to activate and strengthen the third eye. Meditation will allow you to develop the desired powers and maintain control over them. Nothing will prevent you from achieving your objectives if you maintain your dedication and concentration.

Internal Awakening To The Universe

When we recline and contemplate the awe-inspiring grandeur of the night sky, we feel minuscule in comparison to the infinite diamond abyss staring at us.
When we see images of spiraling galaxies spanning thousands of light years or learn about the titanic stellar forces that sparked Creation with a

"BANG!", their vastness and complexity appear enigmatic and infinite.

What if, however, I told you that these majestic celestial bodies spinning in the infinite Cosmos are also spinning within you at this very moment? That the planets of the Solar System have a residence within you?

There is a network of channels within your body that provides access to dimensions of reality beyond the physical world. Chakras are the names for these energy points.

Chakras are openings through which energy enters and exits the aura, which is our energy body. We are like organisms in the surrounding energy sea. Each of these vortices is engaged in a continuous energy exchange with the Universal Energy Field. The chakras are genuinely open when we speak of feeling "open"

The term 'Chakra' means 'wheel' in Sanskrit. The term refers to the configuration of the Chakras and their spinning motion when they are healthy and functioning properly. Chakras have been extensively used throughout history, beginning in India during vedic times and spreading to Tibet, China, Nepal, and more recently Western culture through meditation and yoga practice exposure.

Chakras are actually portals within us that connect Heaven and Earth, Mind and Body, Spirit and Matter, and the Past and Future. The vast energy domains of the Chakras contain all possible physical, mental, and spiritual human potential.

This column of the spinal mandala is known as the "Rainbow Bridge" — a symbolic seven-rung staircase that spans Heaven, Earth, and the Underworld. If we wish to accomplish integration and the actualization of our greatest potential in this incarnation, we must traverse the bridge through these seven planes.

However, the Rainbow Bridge is more than just a symbol. It is a living reality on your body's energetic realms. The energy of the heavens exists in a very real sense within these portals within you.

Animated Archetypes

Each of the seven Chakras corresponds to one of our Solar System's seven visible planets. Each Chakra corresponds to the energy and motion of a specific celestial body. To attain totality, we must bring this inner system into balance and allow the energy of each planet to express itself freely and completely within us.

The seven planets are archetypes representing various psychological functions.

Archetypes are aspects of our own unconscious that have been rendered in the "native tongue" of the unconscious, namely symbols. Because of this, our visions appear as they do. If you've ever pondered why your dream doesn't simply speak to you, it's because... it can't. It does not behave like that. It makes use of archetypes. Archetypes are the mind's innate description of itself and its processes.

The energies represented by celestial bodies in the Zodiac are archetypes.

Each of the planets represents a distinct "flavor" of mental energy. Each planet represents a distinct force operating within the human psyche.

Each of these entities is comparable to a "character" in the "play" of our inner world, with its own requirements, strengths, weaknesses, preferences, tendencies, appetites, etc. The Sun, for instance, represents the ego and the conscious consciousness. Mars symbolizes assertiveness and libido. Venus symbolizes the desire to love and to be cherished. The Moon symbolizes our instinctual nature and security requirements. The seven planetary bodies comprise the comprehensive psychological portrait of an individual.

Symbolic power is utilized by archetypes to communicate vast quantities of information to our most fundamental selves. To accurately and exhaustively characterize the energy of Mars through verbal description and organized explanation would require a million books. However, a mythological tale about Mars, the Roman god of conflict, will immediately convey "the whole picture" of this energy.

This is why we read fairy tales to our children and why certain stories have been passed down for millennia, cherished by successive generations. Archetypes are exceptionally effective means of conveying meaning. Because archetypes speak the natural language of the unconscious, the principles and lessons they convey are deeply rooted in the foundation of our minds.

There are, in fact, dimensions of your being that can only be accessed via archetypal language. Your energy body does not comprehend reason and logic; it communicates through symbols. If you have ever attempted to cease an addictive habit by talking and reasoning yourself out of it, you are well aware that the unconscious does not deal in logic or reason. It cannot be persuaded by a persuasive argument. You might as well speak Mandarin to a French person and expect them to comprehend you.

The powers of archetypal symbolism surpass anything that could be accomplished through rational discourse. Your energy body or astral being can be altered, transformed, and healed on levels that logic could never achieve through the use of archetypal symbols.

You cannot use logic to cure a disease, but you can use archetypes to infuse your being with planetary energy. You will be astounded by the effects of this work and your own capacity to heal your mind, body, and spirit by simply opening up to the celestial forces residing in the sky above and deep within your spiritual and etheric bodies.

Each Chakra corresponds to a planet, and you can interact with each Chakra by employing the archetypal symbol of the planet that governs it. The corresponding planet actually resides in that Chakra. Each planet resides in a particular body center. Constantly, these planetary energies influence us from both the outside and the inside.

The Microcosm Internally

Since the advent of time, the concept of planetary energies existing within the human body has been present in numerous spiritual traditions and cultures across the globe.

God created man in His own image, which esoterically implies that man is a living replica of the entire universe.

The Jewish mystics taught that the human body was the Microcosm, or "Little Cosmos," which was patterned after the Macrocosm, or "Great Cosmos."

Sufi mysticism asserts that our comprehension of ourselves includes an understanding of the entire cosmos, as the microcosm and macrocosm are reflections of each other. The macrocosm is understood to be the external, objective universe, while the microcosm represents the internal, subjective world. Each possesses the characteristics of the other. Rumi, a revered Sufi mystic, states, "You are a reflection of the divine beauty that created the universe." Whatever exists in the universe, you are not separate from it. Whatever you request, pursue it within yourself."

"As Above, So Below" is a proverb attributed to the alchemist Hermes Trismegistus. This implies that everything that exists at the macrocosmic level exists at the microcosmic level as well. Everything that occurs in your external environment also occurs within you. Everything on Earth and in your life is mirrored by the constellations in the sky.

In numerous ways, this correspondence has been ritualized. Throughout history, people have constructed temples in the shape of the human body. In most cases, the altar is located in the "head" of the temple, where the mind or center of consciousness would be. Through the laws of correspondence and energetic resonance, the enchantment and spiritual elevation that occurred within the "body" of the temple also occur within the participants' bodies. The Jewish tabernacle, the Egyptian pyramids, and cross-shaped Christian sanctuaries are additional examples of this practice.

In ancient times, astrology was considered a science, and physicians and chemists closely monitored the movements of the constellations in their endeavors.

Similarly, the ancient world's clerics were also anatomists. A practical, scientific understanding of the occult function of the physical body was regarded as part of religious study. It is believed that when alchemists referred to "vessels" in which they conducted experiments and observed magical transformations, they were not referring to scientific apparatus, but rather to the organs and natural processes occurring within the human body.

Ancient clerics and alchemists recognized that the processes occurring within the human body had much to teach us about the universe itself. They perceived the connection between the "without" and "within" nature. They observed that every function of nature was replicated on a lesser scale within the human body. They taught their disciples that to understand man was to understand the heavens, and that every star in the heavens, every element in the earth, and every function in nature was represented by a corresponding substance or activity in the human body.

Your Sacral Chakra May Be Blocked.

Do you have physical, emotional, or spiritual obstacles in your life? In this case, your sacral chakra may be blocked and require healing. The sacral chakra is one of the seven energy centers, or chakras, in our bodies. It is located in the lower abdomen, approximately two inches below the navel and slightly behind the belly button.

This potent energetic vortex is crucial to our relationships, creativity, and perceptions of personal power, sexuality, pleasure, and comfort. When our sacral chakras are blocked or out of balance, we experience anxiety, isolation from others, and the inability to break toxic patterns. This chapter will assist you in recognizing the symptoms of a blocked, feeble, overactive, or unbalanced sacral chakra.

This chapter concludes with an exam to determine whether or not your sacral chakra requires healing.

Congested Sacral Chakra

Svadhisthana, the sacral chakra, is a vital energy center in the body. This chakra, located in the lower abdomen and associated with water, is crucial to your overall health and well-being. However, when the sacral chakra is blocked or out of balance, it can result in negative symptoms, health problems, anxiety, and depression. In addition, it affects your ability to connect and communicate with others and causes digestive and erotic issues.

There are numerous techniques available for clearing and balancing the sacral chakra. Meditation, visualization exercises, dietary adjustments, and massage therapy are typical techniques. By focusing on harmonizing this vital energy center, you reclaim your internal health and well-being.

Signs of an Obstructed Sacral Chakra

The sacral chakra is in charge of our imagination, sexuality, pleasure, and sensuality. The manifestations of an obstructed sacral chakra are creative stagnation, sexual dysfunction, and low self-esteem. In addition to abdominal pain, other symptoms include constipation, urinary infections, and kidney problems. When the sacral chakra is in harmony, we experience creativity, self-assurance, and sexual fulfillment. We are able to freely express our emotions and appreciate healthy relationships.

If you are experiencing any of the aforementioned negative symptoms, there are a few things you can do to unblock your sacral chakra. Carnelian and citrine are useful for unblocking the sacral chakra. You can also use yoga poses such as warrior II and bridge pose to boost your confidence and creativity.

Causes of Sacral Chakra Blockage

Numerous factors contribute to a blocked sacral chakra, but stress, trauma, and excessive concern or anxiety are among the most common. Other potential triggers include relationship conflicts and sexual or interpersonal issues. Some believe childhood trauma or sexual abuse can also result in a blocked sacral chakra.

To unblock and heal your sacral chakra, you must address these underlying causes by relaxing more often, releasing negative emotions such as anger and resentment, seeking better support from friends and family, and making healthy lifestyle choices such as eating a balanced diet and getting enough exercise. Your sacral chakra will return to its natural state of balance and harmony with time and perseverance.

True Account: Tracy's Sacral Chakra Healing

Tracy recently sought assistance for a blocked sacral chakra. She labored for years with symptoms including low self-esteem, sexual dysfunction, and digestive issues. Tracy discovered through consultation with a health practitioner that her issues were likely caused by an imbalanced sacral chakra.

Tracy decided to employ multiple techniques to clear her sacral chakra. She engaged in meditation and visualization exercises, kept an emotional journal, and adopted a more vigorous exercise regimen. After approximately one month of consistent practice, Tracy observed that her sacral chakra had begun to clear, and she felt more confident, creative, and fulfilled.

Know that you are not alone if you are experiencing a blocked sacral chakra. By addressing the root causes of this imbalance, you can begin to naturally cleanse and heal your sacral chakra.

Weak Sacral Chakra

While a blocked sacral chakra can result in numerous negative symptoms and negatively impact your health, wellbeing, and relationships, a feeble sacral chakra can also be problematic. A weak sacral chakra disconnects you from your emotions, resulting in indifference or solitude. You may also find it challenging to openly convey your emotions or pursue creative endeavors.

In addition, a feeble sacral chakra increases your risk of digestive disorders, menstrual issues, infertility, and low libido. It can also increase your susceptibility to addiction, as you may seek solace in substances or activities.

Signs of an Imbalanced Sacral Chakra

If your sacral chakra is weak, you may experience anxiety, mood swings, difficulty focusing on duties at hand, difficulty managing stress, and apathy, among other symptoms. In addition, a sluggish sacral chakra causes physical issues such as digestive problems, POTS (postural orthostatic tachycardia syndrome), low energy levels, and frequent infections.

Suppose you struggle with these or other symptoms associated with the sacral chakra. In such a case, it is essential to seek the assistance of a trained healthcare professional who can assist you in addressing underlying causes and restoring chakra system balance. You can regain your strength and creativity and find pleasure in living life to its fullest potential with proper care and attention.

Reasons Behind a Weak Sacral Chakra

As with an obstructed or overactive sacral chakra, a weak sacral chakra has multiple possible causes. These include childhood trauma or abuse, a negative outlook on sexuality or intimate relationships, and excessive stress and anxiety. A poor diet and certain medications or medical treatments can also contribute to a feeble sacral chakra.

To restore balance to your sacral chakra, it is crucial to identify the underlying causes and resolve them with the assistance of a trained professional. In certain instances, this necessitates therapy or counseling to overcome past traumas. In other instances, simple lifestyle modifications, such as consuming a more balanced diet and engaging in regular physical activity, are sufficient to support the sacral chakra and promote healing.

The Healing of Maria's Sacral Chakra in Real Life

Maria had been experiencing symptoms of a diminished sacral chakra for several years. She had always felt emotionally detached from others and struggled to connect with her creativity. Over time, these emotions also affected her health. Maria realized she suffered from chronic digestive issues and chronic fatigue.

Maria decided to focus on sacral chakra restoration after conducting research and discussing her symptoms with her physician. She began an exercise regimen and ate a nutrient-dense diet consisting of whole cereals, fruits, and vegetables, as well as healthy fats. Within a few months, Maria observed that her digestion had improved, her energy levels had increased, and she felt significantly happier and more emotionally in tune.

Unbalanced Sacral Chakra

The overactive sacral chakra is marked by insecurity, a lack of self-confidence, and an inability to let go of certain emotions or viewpoints. When the sacral chakra is overactive, we feel excessively emotional or sexual, as well as vulnerable to addiction and self-destructive behavior.

If you suspect that your sacral chakra is out of balance, there are steps you can take to restore equilibrium. First, spend time near water bodies such as lakes and oceans. Additionally, you can meditate on the hue orange and wear orange clothing. Eat foods that contain water, such as cucumbers and citrus.

By taking these measures, you assist in restoring balance to your sacral chakra and harmony to your life.

Manifestations of a Hyperactive Sacral Chakra

When one of the chakras becomes overactive, a variety of symptoms manifest. For instance, an overactive root chakra can cause anxiety or insecurity, whereas an underactive solar plexus chakra can lead to digestive difficulties. Also associated with an overactive chakra are insomnia, migraines, and racing thoughts.

If you experience any of these symptoms, it is essential that you seek out a qualified spiritual healer to help you balance your chakras. You can restore mental and physical tranquility with the assistance of a trained professional.

Reasons for a Hyperactive Sacral Chakra

When this energy center is overactive, physical and emotional symptoms such as increased tension, insomnia, low libido, depression, chronic pain, and fluid retention manifest. Engage in activities that help activate and release the body's natural healing energies if you experience any of these symptoms and suspect your sacral chakra is out of balance.

Taking a yoga class or receiving a massage are two basic techniques. These techniques concentrate on stimulating the pelvic region, practicing deep breathing exercises or guided meditations to ground yourself in the present moment of your body, and engaging in creative activities such as painting and journaling.

By reconnecting with your body via these techniques, you can help restore harmony to your sacral chakra and recover your sense of pleasure and vitality.

True Account: Sarah's Sacral Chakra Healing

Sarah labored for several years with an overactive sacral chakra. She had always been a sensitive individual. Sometimes she would become so inundated by her emotions that she would act rashly or lash out at others.

In addition to her emotional difficulties, Sarah also experienced chronic pain and digestive problems. She had visited numerous physicians, but none of them were able to determine the source of her problems.

Sarah, frustrated and despondent, decided to seek out a spiritual healer who specializes in chakra restoration. After several months of consistent energy work and a detoxifying diet, Sarah regained her equilibrium.

Her emotional outbursts subsided, her chronic pain diminished, her energy levels increased, and she felt considerably more optimistic and in harmony with her body. Today, Sarah routinely visits her healer and maintains a healthy lifestyle to maintain a balanced sacral chakra.

Chakra Disharmonie

The sacral chakra governs our creativity, sexuality, and pleasurable perception. This energy center causes physical, mental, and emotional symptoms when it is out of balance. You experience fatigue, anxiety, or depression and have difficulty concentrating and resting. Your body feels misaligned, and you are experiencing pain or distress.

There are numerous methods to balance your chakras, including meditation, yoga, Tai Chi, and energy work from a certified practitioner. Additionally, crystals and essential fragrances can be used to balance your chakras. You can restore harmony and well-being to your mind, body, and spirit by focusing on balancing your chakras.

Manifestations of an Unbalanced Sacral Chakra

When the sacral chakra is out of balance, it causes a multitude of physical, emotional, and mental symptoms. Chronic pain, diminished libido, digestive issues, and depression are some of the most common indications of an out-of-balance sacral chakra. When the sacral chakra is out of balance, we experience a disconnection with our emotions and desires and find it difficult to express ourselves emotionally. We also experience creative blockage and difficulty enjoying our pastimes and interests.

If you are experiencing any of these symptoms and suspect that your sacral chakra is out of balance, you can restore harmony through a variety of techniques. Spending time in nature, practicing meditation or mindfulness, and engaging in creative pursuits are examples of uncomplicated methods.

Reasons for an Imbalanced Sacral Chakra

There are numerous possible causes of an unbalanced sacral chakra. A lack of physical affection in childhood is a common cause. If you were not given enough embraces or affection as a child, you may have developed feelings of profound insecurity and the conviction that you are unworthy of love. This can inhibit your adult ability to experience delight and creativity.

Trauma, whether sexual, emotional, or physical, is a common cause of sacral chakra imbalance. If you have experienced a traumatic event, it is imperative that you seek professional assistance to restore your wounds. Your sacral chakra will likely become balanced once the traumas have been resolved.

Lastly, suppressing your creativity or sexuality on a consistent basis can also contribute to an imbalanced sacral chakra. If you have been repressing your true desires for a long time, it is crucial that you begin to explore these emotions in order to realign your chakra.

The Healing of Jennie's Sacral Chakra in Real Life

Jennie, a 38-year-old mother of two, has always been an imaginative individual. She has always had a passion for conveying herself artistically through singing, writing, and dancing. Unfortunately, Jennie's career had always taken precedence over her interests, so she rarely had time for them.

Jennie was dissatisfied with this imbalance in her life for years. She felt trapped and miserable, but had no idea how to pursue her creative interests. Eventually, Jennie began seeing a therapist to assist her in coping with her dissatisfaction.

Jennie's therapist helped her recognize, after several months, that she suppressed her creativity in order to cope with low self-esteem. As a child, Jennie's parents and teachers told her she was insufficient, and this lead her to suppress her creativity.

Once Jennie resumed her creative pursuits, she felt more balanced and content. She prioritized her interests and even pursued a vocation in the arts.

Jennie is content and flourishing due to her newly balanced sacral chakra.

Checking the Balance of Your Sacral Chakra – The Quiz

sustaining a balanced chakra system is essential for sustaining mental, physical, and spiritual equilibrium. If you suspect your sacral chakra is out of balance, take this short quiz. Each query has four possible responses; please select the one that best describes you.

How frequently did you receive physical affection from your parents or caregivers as a child?

a) Very often

b) Sometimes

c) Infrequently

d) Never

How do you convey your emotions?

a) I am very frank and forthright about my emotions.

b) I tend to hold my emotions in check.

c) I have difficulty expressing my emotions.

d) I am prone to becoming extremely emotional, even when it may not be appropriate.

What do you think of your creative abilities?

a) I am very assured in my creative abilities and use them frequently in my work and pastimes.

b) I am reasonably assured of my creative abilities and appreciate expressing them in my spare time.

c) I lack confidence in my creative abilities, but I do my best to utilize them in my spare time.

d) I lack confidence in my creative abilities and rarely express that aspect of my personality.

When was the last time you experimented with something novel?

a) Within the previous month.

b) Within the previous year.

c) Greater than one year ago.

d) I do not recollect.

What do you think of your sexuality?

a) I am extremely at ease with my sexuality.

b) I am relatively at ease with my sexuality.

c) I am uneasy with my sexual orientation.

d) I am extremely uneasy with my sexuality.

Do you have any concerns or hang-ups about intimacy?

a) No, I am quite receptive to intimacy.

b) Some, but I am actively striving to overcome them.

c) Yes, I have numerous concerns and hang-ups concerning intimacy.

d) I do not consider intimacy.

How would you characterize your level of energy?

a) High

b) Moderate

c) Low

d) I am unaware of my vitality level.

Do you prefer being with others or being alone?

a) I prefer being around others and become restless when I am alone for too long.

b) I appreciate being in the company of others, but I don't mind spending time alone when necessary.

c) I dislike being around people, but I can tolerate it if necessary.

d) I prefer to be alone and frequently feel exhausted after spending too much time with others.

Are you able to readily let go of things?

a) Yes, extremely readily.

b) It can be challenging at times, depending on the circumstances of my existence.

c) No, I find it difficult to let go of items.

d) It depends on the object I need to relinquish.

Do you live on the spur of the moment or do you plan everything in advance?

a) I am not impulsive and rarely make decisions on the spur of the moment.

b) I attempt to plan things as much as possible, but sometimes I go with my gut.

c) I always attempt to plan things in advance as much as feasible.

d) I do not plan ahead or make decisions on the spur of the moment.

A Guide to the Sacral Chakra

If the majority of your responses were affirmative, your sacral chakra is likely open and balanced. It indicates that you have a healthy sense of originality, sexuality, and self-worth. You probably appreciate trying new things and are satisfied with who you are. You are also at ease in your own skin and appreciate social interaction.

If you answered primarily with Bs to the preceding questions, your sacral chakra is likely open and balanced, but there is room for improvement. It indicates that you likely have a healthy sense of creativity, sexuality, and self-worth, but there are areas in which you could make improvements.

If the majority of your answers to the queries above were Cs, your sacral chakra is likely blocked. It indicates that you may have trouble expressing yourself creatively, feel uneasy around others, have low energy levels, lack motivation, and struggle with intimacy.

If you answered the preceding queries primarily with Ds, your sacral chakra is likely overactive. It indicates that you have excessive or extreme sexual desires, an abundance of creative ideas, and a high level of vitality. You also have difficulty maintaining focus and are easily distracted.

If you are experiencing symptoms of a blocked, out-of-balance, or overactive sacral chakra, it would be beneficial to seek the guidance of a therapist or other professional who can assist you on your path to healing and balance. Whether through meditation, therapy, or other techniques, there are numerous methods to work on healing and opening your sacral chakra in order to regain life balance.

Visualization And Meditation

Meditation is the practice of concentrating on the present moment, thereby preventing the mind from wandering as it normally would. It involves directing your attention to a single object, such as the appearance of a candle flame, your palms, a leaf, your breath, or even a sensation or an emotion. It is about focusing on one thing so that the chatter in your consciousness is silenced, allowing you to connect with the divine energy of life. As you might assume, this is very beneficial for your chakras.

Meditation is a state of mind, body, and spirit in which one focuses on his or her breathing to attain a profound sense of calm and inner peace. It is an easy-to-learn and practice form of self-help that is an invaluable stress reliever that enhances moods and sleep quality.

The only requirements for meditation are your body, your respiration, and a small amount of time every day. Meditation is also known to enhance the attention span of individuals with Attention Deficit Hyperactivity Disorder (ADHD) and reduce heart disease risk factors such as high blood pressure.

Meditation is beneficial for the solar plexus chakra because it helps you focus on what is occurring within your body, mind, and life, as opposed to what is happening around you moment to moment and how to respond to such situations as they arise. Meditation serves to balance both sides of the spectrum, thereby balancing the solar plexus chakra, as inward concentration leaves less time for external concerns.

Meditation can help you overcome impulsive behavior by encouraging you to gaze inward and gain a better understanding of what is going on inside you. This improves your ability to respond appropriately rather than reflexively to the surrounding environment.

What Exactly is Visualization?

How does visualization function in conjunction with meditation? The mind is a potent force that can influence every aspect of your existence. How one thinks influences how one feels and what one does in life. When meditation and visualization are combined, they can help create a richer experience for the psyche.

Visualization is merely imagining images as if they are occurring in the present moment. During meditative practice, it can be used to construct scenes around the body that connect its parts to locations on Earth or other planets in our solar system. It is a vital instrument used to energize various points on the body, such as acupuncture points or chakras, for greater balance and insight into self-healing powers.

Guided imagery can also be used as a form of visualization. Guided imagery is a form of narrative that facilitates the visualization of nonexistent or nonexistent objects. These images have a profound effect on the mind and emotions because they activate the mind's innate resources for healing and equilibrium.

One can use visualization in meditation in numerous ways, but one of the most significant is during an empowerment practice. A person is energized by empowerment so that they can pursue new challenges and opportunities in life. If your objective is to accomplish something significant, such as starting a business or attending college, visualize yourself doing it and all that comes with it. At this time, you wish to strengthen your solar plexus chakra, so let's concentrate on that. You are about to receive a set of guided visualization meditations that you can use to work on your solar plexus chakra. I recommend that you record them in your own voice so that you don't have to keep referring back to the book to figure out what you should visualize next, which can break you out of the meditation. Additionally, ensure that you will not be interrupted during these exercises and that you are wearing comfortable clothing.

Visualization Technique for Balancing the Manipura

Now, please settle into the seat you've chosen. Assume a comfortable position in which you can remain for the extent of this visualization. During this meditation, if you discover that you need to make adjustments, that's fine. Do so with care and affection. Here, there is no space for judgment. When you are at ease, you may resume meditation.

When you realize your mind has wandered off to another place, bring it back with compassion. Don't be disappointed in yourself. This is a custom. During this meditation, you may close your eyes or leave them half-open with a gentle, unfocused gaze.

Observe your breath now. Observe the manner in which your chest rises and falls. Observe the natural rhythm of your respiration and simply sit with it. If you observe your mind wandering, you can bring it back to your breath or allow it to return to your solar plexus and remain there.

It's acceptable to have thoughts while sitting. You can allow them to enter and depart at will by simply returning your attention to your meditation. It is now time to breathe. Repeat three times. It makes no difference whether you are gaping or not. Just take three long, satisfying yawns. Have patience with this. There is no need to hurry.

Once you have completed yawning, return your focus to your breath and observe what is occurring. Now, breathe deeply, allowing your abdomen to fill with oxygen first, followed by your lungs. Allow the air to slowly evacuate, and then repeat the process. Out and in. Take another deep breath and focus your attention on the root of your spine.

Imagine you have a red ball of light at the base of your vertebrae. Observe this light as it expands and radiates from within you to the outside world. Observe how the lights illuminate your entire body. Now, shift your focus from the root to the sacral chakra. Observe the orange orb of light and permit it to encircle your entire body. Now shift your focus to your solar plexus. Observe that you possess a small, yellow-glowing light orb. Observe this light's expansion as you inhale. As you exhale, observe how you begin to emit a yellow radiance. Permit this yellow light to envelop your entire abdomen and thorax. Feel it as it spreads across your upper and lower bodies. Recognize that this is the source of your motivation.

This light is the manifestation of your hopes and ambitions. The energy that propels you to fulfill your life's destiny. Feel its warmth and strength as it travels through your entire body, commencing in your abdomen. Observe how it covers your neck, head, and lower body. Feel this yellow energy infusing you with enthusiasm, passion, and joy. Feel your inner self reawakened and prepared to face the challenges of life. With a smile on your countenance, charge forward. As you exhale, experience the relief of knowing that you have already overcome every obstacle that could possibly arise. You may now commence to chant. RAM... RAM... RAM

It is now time to return to your normal breathing pattern. Observe that the yellow radiance continues to surround you. Observe how the light pulsates powerfully from your solar plexus. Observe, with each inhalation, how permeated you are with passion and pleasure for life. Repeat the following affirmations aloud or silently, whichever you prefer:

I feel my personal authority, which is wonderful. I am highly motivated to make my aspirations a reality. I am currently on the path to achieving my destiny. I transform everything I touch into gold. I am accomplished in all of my endeavors. I am aware of what I wish to achieve, and I maintain concentration. Ideas occur to me effortlessly and rapidly. I execute these brilliant concepts with great success. I always observe the outcomes of my efforts. My word is my oath, and I always carry out my commitments. I am always willing to go above and beyond to accomplish my lofty goals. I have a strong belief in what I intend to accomplish. I have complete confidence in myself and my abilities. I pursue my goals with assurance because they are already realized.

Allow this pure yellow light and silence to energize your body, mind, and spirit as you continue to revel in it. Take in this yellow radiance and allow it to energize you. Feel the exhilaration of its movement as it envelops you from head to toe.

Now that we are nearing the conclusion of this visualization, you must exit as slowly as possible. Return your focus to your respiration first. As your chest rises and descends with each inhale and exhale, focus on its rhythm. To bring your awareness completely into your body, wiggle your toes and fingertips gently. You can move your limbs and legs if you wish to feel more grounded in the present. Now, slowly and gingerly open your eyes as you continue to focus on what is occurring energetically within you. Take one more deep breath in and out, and express gratitude for the changes you've just made.

Yellow

Yellow, the color associated with cheerfulness and brightness, is the symbol of sunshine, joy, and optimism. However, this color also has negative connotations, as do all colors. Let's examine this in depth.

Shade of Will

The sun is typically represented by the color yellow, as it is the source of all life on Earth. The idiom "he/she is a star" refers to being similar to the sun. The sun creates and carries out its will for life to flourish on this planet. Yellow represents the archetype of someone's or something's will or intent.

Yellow is commonly associated with positivity, intelligence, enlightenment, vitality, enthusiasm, clarity, and happiness. However, it is also associated with deceit, cowardice, jealousy, illness, and caution (when someone's will is feeble or perverted).

The majority of research conducted on the color indicates that it can increase muscular vitality, mental activity, and happiness. It is also known to activate and strengthen memory and communication, stimulate the nervous system, enhance vision, and boost self-confidence. All of these items can help you carry out your will.

As the mythological planet of transit and the fastest planet in our solar system's orbit around the sun, this hue is commonly associated with the planet Mercury. This explains why many taxicabs, traffic signs, and school buses are yellow.

This appealing color stimulates spontaneous action, which is why it is frequently used in children's toys and other products. Children are also dependent on the will of their parents or others, such as their teachers/coaches. This makes them more receptive to the hue yellow until they develop an independent will. Since it is perceived as a childlike color, marketers often avoid using it when targeting adults.

Yellow is the hue of the third chakra.

The 'Solar Plexus' chakra, known in Sanskrit as the 'manipura' chakra, is the third of your body's seven chakras. 'Mani' refers to pearl and 'pura' means city, so 'manipura' refers to pearls of lucidity, wisdom, and common sense in the population.

Experts also refer to the third chakra as the 'self-power' chakra because, when it is balanced, it regulates and boosts your self-confidence, discipline, and ability to pursue and accomplish all of your goals.

This chakra, located just behind the navel and slightly below the ribcage, is responsible for your physical, emotional, and psychological health and well-being. The color yellow represents the third chakra. Additionally, the third chakra impacts the liver, stomach, pancreas, eyes, face, and large intestines.

When your solar plexus chakra is balanced, you feel just like you do when there is a balance of yellow in your life: energized, alive, joyful, optimistic, fresh, and healthy. Nonetheless, an overactive third chakra causes you to be critical, aggressive, furious, and judgmental, which also occurs when you overuse the color yellow in your life.

In contrast, an underactive manipura chakra causes severe emotional problems and a lack of self-confidence.

To feel healthy, joyful, energized, and focused, it is essential to maintain a balance of yellow in your life, which is one method for balancing your solar plexus chakra.

Yellow has a variety of intriguing meanings in various cultures.

Different Meanings of Yellow In Egypt, the color yellow symbolizes the deceased.

In India, it represents merchants. In Japan, it represents strength and courage. In some traditions, the term 'yellow-bellied' is used to refer to cowardly individuals.

Yellow ribbons are also worn in some cultures as a symbol of optimism and to welcome loved ones. 'Mellow yellow' refers to relaxation. 'Yellow journalism' refers to irresponsible or poor reporting.

Methods For Opening Your Third Eye

Yoga and meditation are excellent methods for opening the third eye, and they never fail if you put in the time, effort, and have pure intentions. However, there are additional methods you can employ to open your third eye quicker. Consider them spiritual supplements that lead inexorably to the correct energy flow through your chakras and, consequently, a healthy energy body. Let's begin by examining one of the most common alternative techniques for opening the Ajna.

Mindfulness

Mindfulness entails being completely present in the present moment. It is a rare individual who does not dwell on the past or fret about the future. This is not to say that everyone does not experience some degree of mindfulness on a daily basis, but this is not typically a deliberate state of being. When you're having a good time with your loved ones or doing something you've always desired to do, you may experience flow. You are certain that one of these experiences will be one of the images that flash before your eyes in your final moments before moving on to the next magnificent adventure that life has to offer.

Mindfulness requires awareness of where you are and what is occurring. It involves being entirely immersed in what you're doing, noticing what's happening in your space, and being firmly rooted in the present moment. There is neither the time nor the energy to be concerned, anxious, or fearful in this state of mind. You are present in your eternal splendor in its entirety. You are in touch with your true nature.

Since the mind is frequently "pinging all over the place," you must continually bring yourself back to the present. If you're not careful, the next thing you know, you're worrying about paying the mortgage, the upcoming expenses, or something regrettable that happened in the past that you wish you had handled differently.

There are numerous methods for practicing mindfulness. You can practice mindfulness while standing, walking, sitting, or simply moving your body in any manner that feels natural. Mindfulness can also be practiced by intentionally halting throughout the day to be present. You could incorporate mindfulness meditation if you enjoy sports, working out, or performing yoga, for example. It's all about being very present, conscious of your respiration and body movements.

Some individuals mistakenly believe that mindfulness is an internal process. For these individuals, meditation and mindfulness involve focusing on their thoughts and determining what they are thinking. If you approach mindfulness and meditation in this manner, you may feel as if your body is a heavy bag of flesh and bones that is a burden you do not need. When you begin to consider mindfulness in terms of the body as well as the mind, you will begin to access levels of energy flow that are beyond your fondest imagination.

Engaging in Mindful Meditation

Sitting is the first step in proper mindfulness meditation. You must ensure that your body is in a comfortable position in order to concentrate on sensations, respiration, etc., without being distracted by discomfort. Therefore, when beginning a meditation practice, you must take time to become stable and centered. If you have physical issues or injuries, you can make the necessary adjustments.

Utilize an appropriate chair, a park bench, or a floor cushion for seating. Whatever option you select, it must be sturdy and stable.

Take note of what your extremities are doing. You must guarantee that the soles of your feet are flat on the floor when seated in a chair. Make sure your legs are extended out in front of you and crossed if you're sitting on a cushion. Again, if this is not suitable, you must ensure that you are sitting up straight and that you are not experiencing any discomfort.

Now, concentrate on your upper body. Ensure that it is as straight as possible without feeling rigid. You should maintain a natural curve in your spine, so avoid exerting yourself to the point where it feels unnatural. Your head and shoulders should rest atop your vertebrae comfortably.

Now is the time to observe the position of your upper limbs in relation to your upper body. Both arms should be parallel to the torso. If you let your arms descend naturally to your sides, they will be in the correct position. You will discover yourself slouching if they are too far forward. If they are too far back, your upper back and shoulders will become rigid. Therefore, avert your eyes if you need to truly connect with how your body feels in order to properly position yourself. Again, you must be as upright as possible while remaining at ease and calm.

Let's move on to what is occurring within your mind. Your chin should be slightly lowered toward your torso, and your eye line should be gently sloping. You may allow your eyelids to fall if you wish, but it is not required. People believe your eyes must always be closed during meditation, but this is not always the case. Simply allow whatever feels natural to your eyes to occur.

Now that your body is in the correct position, you may simply unwind and enjoy the present moment. Concentrate on your breathing. Observe it as it enters, touches your nostrils, and descends into your lungs. Feel it flood your stomach and lungs. Pay close attention to your breath as it travels from your abdomen to your nostrils. Perceive your body adjusting to the exhale.

When your mind wanders away from your breathing — and it will — simply acknowledge that you've been distracted, be grateful that you've noticed, and bring it back to the present moment in a gentle, compassionate manner. You should never punish yourself for becoming distracted, even if it occurs sixty times per minute. This would be counterproductive to the mindfulness practice and would certainly not benefit your third eye. Simply restore your attention to your breath when your mind wanders.

That is mindfulness in a nutshell. This exercise can be performed while seated, strolling, or standing. As you breathe, pay attention to how your body feels and its posture when you are standing, as well as your connection to the earth. Observe how your body feels with each step you take while walking and attempt to synchronize your breathing with each stride.

Crystals

Crystals are remarkable instruments for awakening the third eye. Let's take a peek at the most useful stones.

For good reason, amethyst is dubbed the Stone of Spirituality. It enhances the function of the third eye chakra and can aid in spiritual development. Using this chakra stone, you will not only awaken the Ajna, but also strengthen your connection to your intuition and psyche, and acquire psychic abilities.

Meditation with amethyst is beneficial because it enables you to access even deeper levels of consciousness, allowing you to comprehend all of life's challenges in greater depth. Using this stone will also assist you in gaining clarity and making sound decisions. It is a stone that can help you stop having nightmares, recall your visions, and sleep more soundly.

Ametrine is a combination of citrine and amethyst, and it aids in connecting with your higher self and discovering your personal strength. As it opens up your brow energy center, you will become aware of your limiting beliefs. As it serves to open your third eye, you will begin to comprehend the underlying causes of your problems. In addition, this stone is beneficial for migraines.

Labradorite is also known as the Magic Stone. This mysterious stone facilitates communication with the supernatural world. As you meditate with this stone and wear it as adornment, your third eye will respond to it. You will begin to recognize your psychic abilities, and your intuition will develop. Those who utilize it experience recollection of past lives, prophecy, telepathy, channeling, and clairvoyance. In addition, it helps your aura become more protective, isolating you from energies that are harmful or lower your frequency. When you are vibrating at low frequencies, you experience dreadful mental, physical, and emotional distress, which impacts your third eye and causes it to close once more. Use this stone to help you stimulate your imagination, find calm and boost your intellect. It does marvels for your brain, metabolism, and eyes, and helps you discover your purpose.

Lepidolite is a stress-relieving stone that reduces the propensity to overthink or mistrust oneself. You can place this stone on your third eye and meditate, allowing its consciousness to communicate with yours so that it can assist you in removing the emotional and energetic blocks that prevent your third eye from functioning properly.

Lapis Lazuli is the Stone of Illumination and Enlightenment. The consciousness of this stone will interact with your third eye. In particular, it enhances psychic intuition and rationality. The greater your use of this stone, the greater the flow of prana through your Ajna, the higher your frequency, and the heightened your awareness of the spiritual domain. In addition to reducing insomnia, enhancing dream recall, and enhancing brain and eye function, this stone is remarkable for its ability to enhance brain and eye function.

Tourmalinated Quartz is an exquisite blend of spiritual and earthly vitality. In other words, it helps you establish a connection with your psychic nature while ensuring that you remain grounded. Some individuals have a tendency to connect with the spiritual world with their minds in the clouds, which is problematic given that we all reside on earth and must be grounded in order to function properly here. Consequently, this stone is beneficial when experiencing psychic phenomena and losing contact with the physical world.

Sodalite is a stone that can help you connect with your authentic self, embrace yourself, and boost your self-esteem and self-confidence. When using this stone, you will gain clarity, objectivity, and heightened intuition. In addition, it assists you in finding a balance between your emotions and your beliefs. Use this stone to counteract distractions, negative thoughts, and tension.

Blue Tiger's Eye is an excellent stone for enhancing self-awareness, as it brings to the surface issues that must be resolved. Until you resolve certain issues, it will be difficult to activate your third eye, as repressed emotions and experiences can create energetic blockages in this center. Therefore, if you utilize this stone, you will be forced to confront your past emotional traumas in order to heal them. Utilize this stone to stabilize your dispersed energies and emotions, heighten your psychic abilities, and enhance your clairvoyance. Expect this to also improve your mental lucidity, alleviate your depression, and assist you in recognizing your own worth.

The Hag Stone is a potent stone for safeguarding the spiritual and emotional vitality of the Ajna. It protects you from psychic attacks and prevents you from imbibing negative energy. Utilizing this throughout your meditation and visualization sessions will facilitate the formation of mental images. Additionally, it offers protection against visions.

In addition to helping you connect with your personal protectors, angels, and ascended masters, Blue Quartz will also open your third eye chakra. The energy of this stone is profoundly tranquil, and it encourages spiritual receptivity.

Kyanite is a beneficial stone that promotes self-discovery, alterations in perception from the visible to the invisible, and the awakening of other senses. Utilize this stone to enhance your meditation and increase the flow of prana to your brow chakra.

Blue Apatite facilitates access to the Akashic records, past life regression, and deeper connections to consciousness than ever before. In addition to aiding in objective attainment, this stone eliminates apathy and confusion. It can facilitate problem-solving creativity and learning. You will notice that your psychic abilities are growing increasingly potent.

Black Obsidian is a grounding stone that facilitates personal transformation through shadow work, past life work, and karma healing. Occasionally, we bring with us baggage from prior lives that must be eliminated before our energy centers can function properly. With the Stone of Truth, you will find yourself introspecting in order to bring to light everything you've concealed in the shadows, heal it, and evolve into a grander, superior version of yourself. It is also useful for communicating with spirit guides.

Essential Oils

Using essential oils to balance your energy centers is a highly effective method. Since chakras are energy vortices, essential oils possess their own energetic frequencies that can influence the functioning of these energy centers.

Patchouli essential oil is a fantastic oil for the third eye. This oil grows better with age, which is a wonderful characteristic. You can apply this topically to combat depression, improve your mood, and increase your libido. Utilize this oil during meditation to improve the passage of energy through the Ajna chakra.

Since ancient times, frankincense essential oil has always been beneficial. In the Bible, it was a present given to Jesus at his birth. Frankincense derives from the resin of the Boswellia tree. It has a soothing, calming effect on your mind, body, and spirit and can assist you in overcoming your concerns and anxieties. When you use this during meditation, you will have greater clarity, access to your third eye's abilities, and enhanced intuition.

Lavender is a highly adaptable essential oil, and one of the finest you can use for psychic development. Additionally, it is excellent for relieving depression, anxiety, and tension. When you're not dealing with these issues, it's much simpler to open your third eye, and there are no longer any blockages that can prevent the energy from flowing, allowing you to access higher spiritual realms. Another amazing aspect of lavender is that it is inexpensive. Use lavender to treat mental health issues, the flu, the common cold, and even skin irritations. Use this essential oil to help you open your third eye during meditation.

Cedarwood is an excellent oil for connecting with nature. The closer you are to nature, the more your energy centers are stimulated, and the more likely it is that you will be able to open your third eye chakra. This oil promotes yin and yang balance and transports you to the vast outdoors. You can use this product on your hair and epidermis, and you'll enjoy the aroma. During your meditation, you can place this oil in a diffuser so that you can scent it and allow it to work its magic on your Ajna chakra.

Clary Sage oil is ideal for removing low-vibration energies and emotions. This allows you to purify your aura and mind, making it simpler for prana to flow through all of your chakras and nadis. In addition to opening you up to psychic experiences, meditating with this oil will provide you with clarity, calm, and a general sense of well-being. This can help you obtain clarity when making difficult decisions. Use this in a diffuser during meditation, or apply it to your skin as a perfume.

German chamomile, which is calming, gentle, and connects you to nature, and rose, which grounds you, settles you down, and aligns your spirit, body, and mind, are two additional essential oils. Blends of these essential oils can be utilized to expedite psychic activation.

Dream Journaling

This is an effective method for awakening the third eye. When you dream or have an out-of-body experience, the third eye is the primary energy center at work, allowing you to perceive these experiences in a world beyond or within this one. Some individuals are unable to recall their visions, while others claim they never dream. Nevertheless, everyone dreams. If you disagree, or if you never recollect your dreams, I will explain how to change that. Important to note is that the more deliberate you are about recalling your dreams, the more you will be able to remember and the more active your third eye will be. The best method to remember your dreams is to record them in a dream journal, the princess of dream recall. Ensure that you do this routinely, even if you have excellent dream recall.

Put a pen and notebook beside your bed at all times. You can obtain a dream journal app or simply use your phone's voice recording app if you're not inclined to go old school.

Before falling asleep, ensure your comfort and declare out loud that you will recollect your dreams. This statement can be repeated endlessly until you fall unconscious.

Do not move and do not open your eyes when you awaken. Do not contemplate the tasks you must complete for the day.

Recall the last detail of your dream, even if it was only a color, a taste, or a sensation. If you cannot recall any images, contemplate how you felt.

Retrace your steps backward. In other words, don't attempt to remember everything from when your dream began; instead, start with what happened before you woke up, then what happened before that, etc., until you can no longer recall anything.

Note everything that you can recall. Again, do not berate yourself if all you can recall is how you felt when you awoke.

As you go about your day, you may encounter circumstances that stimulate your memory of a dream-related experience. Include this in your journal. Ensure that you affirm every night that you will remember your visions, and you will achieve excellent results. Before going to sleep, it is also beneficial to recall the entire day. Start by considering what you were doing immediately before turning out the lights and retiring for the night, and then proceed backwards.

Visible Dreaming

A lucid dream is one in which the dreamer is aware that they are fantasizing. Instead of awakening from your dream, you can take control of the situation. You will observe that everything in the dream world is susceptible to your thoughts and emotions, and you can control what transpires through your intention. People become impatient and abandon their plans before they've had a chance to play out because events in the actual world must occur through the mediums of space and time.

If you wish to learn how to lucid dream, you will find that keeping a dream journal is an indispensable instrument. In addition, the more you practice, the more you will begin to experience psychic phenomena in real life, which indicates that your third eye is now awake. Utilizing reality checks throughout the day will help you accomplish lucidity in your dreams. Configure the alarm to sound on the hour. When the alarm sounds,

Press a finger into the palm of the opposing hand to determine if it emerges on the opposite side of your hand.

Try pushing your hand through a wall by pressing it against it.

Consider whether you are hallucinating.

Try to leap and hover in the air for a few seconds. Don't consider how; just act.

Consider the time, then gaze away and then back. Has it evolved? You are in a fantasy.

Read something, then look aside and then return to it. If the text is different, then you are imagining.

Observe yourself in a mirror and your reflection. If it behaves differently or is distorted, you are dreaming.

The letter A should be written on your palms. Whenever you see this, perform a reality check. This practice will eventually affect your visions.

Examine your digits. Are they finished? Have you some extras? You are in a fantasy.

Ask yourself what you were doing a few moments ago, and track your actions as far back as feasible. If you're doing this in a dream, you'll eventually realize you have no explanation for why or how you're firing at an army of gargoyles while standing next to Sterling Archer in a space pod.

Sadhguru's Methods

Sadhguru discusses two distinct methods for opening the third vision. In reference to this, he stated that Shiva is only remembered for opening his own Ajna, and not for dancing, marrying twice, or meditating. The instant he opened his third eye, he acquired access to all knowledge. Sadhguru asserts that Shiva can perceive things that other humans cannot, which represents the pinnacle of knowledge.

It is said that when Shiva opened his third eye, fire emanated from it, symbolizing the fact that he had destroyed everything he once cherished and valued. The ash, perspiration, and blood that followed the fire indicate that he eradicated every last vestige of ignorance, including everything we accept as true and incontrovertible. He was able to uncover his third eye as a result of his actions.

Therefore, the first method Sadhguru discusses is emptying one's interior so that nothing remains but a vacuum or black void. This black hole devours the entrance to your Ajna, forcing it to divide wide open. In other words, it is doing the same thing Shiva did when he got rid of everything he deemed significant, including his emotions, beliefs, possessions, relationships, and his very essence.

The second method recommended by Sadhguru differs from the first in that, whereas the first method involves burning everything up, this method involves storing everything within yourself. In other terms, neither your emotions nor your thoughts are expressed. You don't even communicate. He claims that if you can remain silent for four days, you will have a sudden inclination to sing or speak on the fifth day because everything inside you will be aching to be expressed. However, if you don't release it, the pressure will build up to the point where your third eye will open.

Getting Ready for Guided Meditation

Experiencing the chakras is not like dieting or exercising. They lack any scientific limitations. It is a spiritual process that transcends the human understanding of time.

The opening of any chakra is not contingent on a time limit, the number of hours invested, or a precise technique. It may take a while to awaken or open the chakra, or it may open on the first try.

The chakra awakening procedure cannot be rushed. Intense desire to activate the Chakra can result in a blockage. You would not go to the gym to get in shape without first making preparations, such as finding the appropriate gym and acquiring the proper equipment.

Activating or awakening chakras requires additional preparation. The initial requirement is an openness to the universe. Accept spirituality and the Divine Energy that pervades the universe.

The capacity to open or awaken your chakras is contingent upon your willingness to do so! Only when you have adopted your spirituality will you be able to connect with your inner energy!

Preparation

You must prepare your mind, body, and spirit for a period of calm reflection. Attempting guided meditation when you are unprepared is analogous to attempting to fall slumber when your mind is restless. You will stir and turn, become frustrated, and then either give up or fall asleep restlessly. The following day, you will feel uncomfortable, exhausted, irritable, and likely have a headache.

Meditation can have the same effect as a difficult or restless night's slumber. You will enjoy the experience more if you make some preparations and get ready for it. You will also experience the benefits, even minor ones, much more quickly.

Acquire Knowledge

If you have never meditated before or interacted with your interior energies, the first time you open that door can be quite a shock. You must be physically, emotionally, and mentally prepared before proceeding. In the modern world, we have access to vast amounts of information. The first key to unleashing your readiness to align with your chakras is information.

Various qualities and behavioral characteristics are affiliated with each chakra. You must become familiar with them and understand the forces behind each chakra. Learn what fears can impede them and the symptoms of each chakra's blockage.

Learn about each Chakra, including its color, element, mudra, vibrations, chain position, and function. Understanding each Chakra will allow you to better concentrate and direct the required energy, color, or element.

Determine the Problem

The only way to remedy a problem is to address its root cause, not just the symptom. As the problem worsens, symptoms tend to recur or even present themselves as new symptoms. Identifying the underlying cause of a problem eliminates its symptoms.

When one bodily process begins to fail, the body will attempt to adjust and reallocate its resources. As the body's resources become depleted, it will begin to malfunction in other areas if the issue is not resolved.

The chakra system functions similarly with energy. If one of the chakras in the chain becomes dysfunctional or obstructed, it will affect the other chakras. If there is an obstruction in one of the chakras, it may be difficult to determine which one it is. Especially if the issue has been ignored for an extended period of time or has never been addressed.

There are several methods to determine which chakra requires attention:

Exists physical pain?

If so, where can I find it?

Does it correspond to one of the chakras?

How do you currently feel emotionally?

What's going on with your relationships?

Which areas of your existence are causing you the most difficulty right now?

When you close your eyes, do you see a specific hue?

Stimulate the Energy of the Chakras

Each Chakra is associated with specific aspects of the body, nature, and the outside universe. If you are attempting to activate or unblock one or more chakras, you must be aware of these characteristics.

Once you grasp the chakras and which energy centers require attention, you can stimulate them by:

Stones and crystals — The corresponding crystal or stone can be worn as ornamentation. Use it while sleeping, during guided meditation, or even during yoga.

Exercise — Perform exercises that stimulate the respective chakra in order to bring it to the forefront during meditation.

Food — Consume the foods and herbal beverages associated with the respective chakra.

Incense or scented candles infused with the fragrances that awaken the chakra should be burned.

Plants — Decorate the room, home, or workplace with flowers and plants associated with the chakra.

Massage — Determine which pressure points stimulate each chakra, or locate a Healing Hands massage therapist who can assist with clearing the channels.

Quiet introspection — Spend some time in solitude contemplating your issues, maladies, and relationships. Examine them intently and attempt to determine what is holding you back or causing you concern.

Advice For Harmonizing Your Sacral Chakra

Sacral Chakra:

The Sacral Chakra embodies sexuality, self-respect, inventiveness, pleasures, and disappointments. It is also known as the Swadhistana or the Second Chakra, and in martial arts as the "Hara." The Second Chakra is located in the lower abdomen, just below the coccyx or tailbone. In addition, its element is water, and its chakra color is orange. This spiritual power center is associated with emotional response regulation. In addition, the second chakra controls the sense of flavor as well as the reproductive functions. As a result of its close proximity to the reproductive organ, this chakra is also a pleasure center. This pleasure may be sensual or of a different nature. In addition, the Swadhistana administers life lessons such as accusing and coercion, sex, power, and control; this Chakra is the foundation of your profound quality of emotion. Additionally, the information stored in this Chakra includes your emotions and feelings, as well as sensations of duality. Therefore, it is also known as the "emotional center." In addition to this, Swadhistan also emanates attractiveness and hospitality.

For health, erotic energies, processing, and sanitization, this energy can therefore be used for creativity and profound mindfulness. It also impacts our sense of self-worth.

Variations in the Sacral Chakra

When a Chakra is blocked, a discrepancy is initially created. Unfortunately, blockages in the second chakra can cause both physical and mental issues. Moreover, the chakras can generate obstructions that diminish the flow of energy. Therefore, it is essential to correct the chakra's imbalance.

Chakras can be blocked in either an overactive or underactive manner. Both of these conditions have numerous and varied effects. Some of the problems that are induced by these problems are as follows.

Psychological instability

increased reliance on others

Relationships characterized by dependence and clinginess

Constriction and abdominal discomfort

incapacity for originality

Females with multiple physical abnormalities.

Tips for Eliminating Sacral Chakra Disparities:

In order to regain one's lost emotional fortitude, one must eliminate all sacral chakra-based imbalances. In addition, one can ensure their physical and mental safety by engaging in activities that are conducive to removing the sacral chakra. The following are some of the guidelines and techniques used to eliminate sacral chakra disparities:

Hip opening yoga postures:

It is commonly believed that our emotional and physical tension is stored in the pelvis. Therefore, the majority of yoga instructors recommend hip-opening postures to relieve tension. Consequently, it is directly related to the sacral chakra. During times of tension or mental exhaustion, pay attention to the sore muscles in your body. Typically, the pharynx is affected. Although the ideal case requires multiple hip-opening postures, it is possible in the early phases to maintain a single posture and release all fatigues and tensions.

Meditation

Meditation is extraordinarily beneficial for cleansing and balancing the chakras. In a typical sacral chakra balancing, for instance, an orange lotus or orange crescent moon is visualized in the pelvic region. Hold this image in your mind for a while and continue to breathe repeatedly.

Utilization of water as the elemental second chakra

As water is a component of the sacral chakra, relaxing near immense bodies of water can help to activate the second chakra. The ocean, waterways, streams, and lakes can aid in chakra activation. Furthermore, if possible, place your feet in the water to allow the energy to circulate through your body. Washing up or taking a shower can also assist in balancing the second chakra.

Learn to release

Above all else, it is essential to learn how to let go of negative emotions. All the people and memories that bring nothing but misery must be abandoned. When we learn how to let go of the things we don't have to convey, we make room for new and improved opportunities.

It may appear simple to sever all emotional attachments and begin a life of isolation, but it is not humanly possible. However, once a person has mastered the discipline of letting go, life becomes simple. We gain the ability to trust our intuition without being governed by our emotions. We take control of our own destinies. Although these tasks are difficult and require practice, they are absolutely worthwhile.

As if no one were observing you, dance.

Dancing is one of the best and simplest methods to open the sacral chakra. Close all the doors and dance like there is no tomorrow if you feel disoriented. In addition, turn on your favorite music and let loose. This activity will provide you with a hip opener.

Other than these techniques, there are few others that effectively eliminate sacral chakra imbalances. These techniques consist of:

Use medicinal substances

Commence using restorative foods

Chakra restorative stones can also be purchased.

The Electrical Aspects Of Rrofound Discovery

When individuals embark on a journey of self-discovery, they typically concentrate on the physical and emotional aspects of their identity. Rarely do people consider the significance of profound self-exposure, despite the fact that they distinguish an otherworldly aspect of their identity. When we investigate the part of our mind that we sometimes refer to as soul or soul, we discover a unique and distinctive aspect of our identity that we may not have known existed.

The travel

We are individuals with physical, profound, educated, and passionate dimensions. We experience the world and the interactions we have on the planet by examining them through these measurements. This is not recent.

We recognize that humans have always considered these measurements. Roman and Greek astrology, Roman horoscopes, and ancient religions are all evidence of the genuine role that otherworldly life has played in human evolution.

The moment we witness a heavenly dawn or an awe-inspiring display of nature that leaves us in a state of bewilderment and awe, realizing there are things in our lives that are beyond our ability to control, may be the moment when we realize there are things beyond our control. We have a conscious or unconscious desire to comprehend this force, which we can refer to as a profound sense of being.

When individuals consider extraterrestrial wellbeing, they typically consider God. Who or whatever they perceive "him" to be. Others consider him to be the antagonistic father figure "the man urstairs" Others reject the concept of any kind of being and find their extraterrestrial existence on earth or in nature.

Then, how would we discover the core of our identities? Some people find it through formal religion, others through yoga or other forms of contemplation that cause them to concentrate on themselves, and still others through a journey of self-disclosure, which they refer to as a religious experience.

Some have compared this profound awakening to a urlifted encountering sensation. As we allow our internal identities to experience life on a more profound level than what is immediately apparent around us, we begin to identify with things differently.

When we focus on otherworldly mindfulness, regardless of how we choose to comprehend the profound side of our identity, we typically discover that we identify ur as a part of our identity, which impacts how we identify with ourselves and others.

The Sacral Chakra, the second chakra.

(Also known as Svadhishthana and Earth Palace)

"Rely only on motion. Life takes place on the level of events, not words. Trust movement." /Alfred Adler/

Location

This chakra is located in the lower abdominal, a few inches below the navel. In males, this chakra is associated with the prostate gland, whereas in women, it is associated with the uterus.

Diversity and presentation

This chakra is typically depicted as orange and in the shape of a six-petalled lotus flower or a vortex, symbolizing the interaction between Earth's energy and the energy of heaven that enters when you breathe consciously. Water is the element of this chakra.

Description

When the root chakra is unblocked and no longer preoccupied with survival, the sacral chakra begins to seek enjoyment, passion, and pleasure. It is said that the sacral chakra is where the energy of the Earth, which enters through the root chakra, meets the energy from divinity. It protects the body from toxins by stimulating the kidneys and lower abdomen, and rids the body of stress and tension, which frequently have profoundly rooted causes. Due to the interaction between the two energies, the sacral chakra functions as a vortex that infuses the body with passion and calms the mind. It controls an individual's sexual vitality. A person with a healthy sacral chakra possesses grounded intuition, a charitable and maternal affection for others, a zest for life, and an abundance of energy that propels them toward their goals and destiny. The sacral chakra is the realm of emotions and sensations, which are frequently best expressed through movement, such as dancing, rather than words.

What occurs when this chakra is deficient?

A healthy sacral chakra enables a person to freely and uninhibitedly express their feelings, emotions, and sexuality. Often through no fault of our own, but due to the conditioning we experience in many societies, we are taught that suppressing your feelings out of fear of losing control is a good thing, which can disconnect us from our bodies, which frequently express our true feelings and trapped emotions. In the majority of Western societies, contradictory sexuality-related beliefs have an effect on the sacral chakra. The sacral chakra expresses not only our sexuality but also our creativity, which is frequently a higher expression of our sexuality or life force. A mundane, unfulfilling job can also contribute to the clogging of your sacral chakra. If you find it simple to open up to others and discuss your sexuality, it may be an indication that your sacral chakra is under-active and requires stimulation.

What occurs if this chakra becomes overactive?
On the opposite end of the spectrum, if the sacral chakra is overactive, you may become overly attached to others, constantly emotional, and even very sexual. You may find yourself constantly surrounded by drama, and you may cultivate dysfunctional relationships, which may cause you to view people as sexual objects for your pleasure. You may experience extreme mood

fluctuations and feel emotions more intensely than you should, leading to the development of unhealthy personal boundaries that make you either extremely dependent on others or even obsessive. You may also exhibit hostility, anxiety, and haughtiness. You may experience cysts, gynecological issues, lower back pain, and kidney problems on a physical level. You may experience an excessively heated abdomen.

How can one cleanse and clear the sacral chakra?
Developing self-awareness is the first stage in healing the sacral chakra, or any chakra for that matter. Once you recognize that you have difficulty expressing your true emotions or that you do so excessively, you can begin to query your habits and beliefs in order to alter unhealthy behaviors. It's possible that these have deep roots, particularly in terms of sexuality, such as bad sexual experiences in the past that have left you scarred. If you have difficulty expressing your emotions, consider creative

activities such as painting or drawing. Don't stress about what you're drawing or whether you can draw; just experiment with different colors and see where they lead you! Dancing is another method to stimulate the sacral chakra and release repressed emotions; if you've never danced before, consider taking a Zumba class for fun. As water is the element of the sacral chakra, being near a lake or river or swimming in a pool can all help to balance the sacral chakra. If your sacral chakra needs to be opened, consider wearing orange hues. If it is overactive, consider wearing the color's opposite, blue. Accepting and nourishing your body in a healthy manner is an additional method for healing the sacral chakra.

Asanas for sacral chakra stimulation

The most effective yoga poses for cleansing the sacral chakra are those that focus on the lower abdomen or pelvis. As opposed to physical exertion, these poses require relaxation. Try the Dancer's pose by beginning in Mountain

Pose, then grabbing your left ankle with your left arm and lifting your left knee toward your buttocks. Reach your right arm forward and maintain this position for several full breaths. Continue on the reverse side.

Additionally, you can stimulate the sacral chakra by performing a simple sun salutation routine five times each morning when you wake up, taking care to move slowly and connect the practice to your respiration.

Meditation
Imagine the breath entering your body through your back as you inhale during meditation, and feel the energy curling as it enters your lower abdomen. As you exhale, visualize the same energy spiraling outward. You can also attempt the hand gesture by stacking your hands (with the left hand underneath the right) and placing them on your lap with the palms facing up. Permit the tips of your

fingertips to make contact. Additionally, you may desire to chant the sound VAM.

Diet & Nutrition

First and foremost, consume plenty of water and stay hydrated so that your body is cleansed and can expel toxins easily. Try consuming citrus fruits, such as oranges, and other sweet fruits, such as coconut and melon. Consider adding cinnamon to your beloved desserts.

Chakra Types in Chapter 2

Although it is said that every expert or teacher has his preferred chakra, there are seven fundamental chakra types. These seven are the primary energy centers in the human organism. A person can become unwell if every transfer or transmission in any of these seven chakras is blocked. Consequently, understanding the location and characteristics of each chakra is essential.

Root Chakra

According to its designation, this chakra represents our foundation and enables us to feel stable. The root chakra represents an individual's foundation. It is situated close to the tailbone and the base of the vertebrae. It regulates emotional regions that revolve around money, basic necessities, and financial matters.

Supreme Chakra

This chakra is concerned with sentiments of exploration and novelty. It aids in preparing an individual to embrace or reject a new experience. It establishes relationships. This chakra is located in the lower abdomen, close to the navel. According to reports, it is two inches below the epidermis and two inches below the navel. It regulates the emotional aspects of sexual desire, pleasure, contentment, and well-being.

Solar Plexus Chakra

This chakra is concerned with a person's capacity to control and be confident in his life. It is located near the intestines in the abdomen. It regulates feelings of self-respect, self-confidence, and self-worth.

Throat Chakra

This chakra relates to the emotions of affection. It determines a person's capacity for altruism. It is located close to the heart in a person's thorax. It controls feelings of love, inner calm, and happiness.

Tongue Chakra

This chakra is located in the pharynx and is responsible for a person's ability to communicate. It regulates the emotions associated with communicating with others, feeling surrounded, expressing oneself, and telling the truth.

Eyebrow Chakra

This chakra relates to a person's capacity to comprehend all aspects of a situation, analyze the larger picture, and maintain concentration. This chakra is sometimes referred to as the brow chakra due to its location near the eyebrows. It is said to be located between the two eyebrows on the forehead. It regulates intellectual reasoning, decision-making ability, wisdom, and intuition.

Throat Chakra

This chakra is the chakra with the highest level in the human organism. It enables a person to have a complete connection with his psyche and leads to complete spirituality. It is located at the crown of the head and regulates the areas of experiencing bliss, connecting heart and spirit, and recognizing inner beauty in addition to physical beauty.

Clearly, each chakra has its own unique function. They begin at the base of the spine and ascend to the crown of the cranium; the location of each chakra corresponds to its function.

How to Activate Your Chakras Chapter 3
Since chakras pertain to your energy system, you must assess the quality of your energy and the health of your system. There exist a number of methods for this purpose. Before doing something that would impair the functionality of your body's system, it is vital to have a thorough understanding of that system. If the system is not correctly maintained, the results will be

subpar, and it may even be harmful to the body.

The most essential aspect is to activate your body's energy system and locate your chakras. Chakras can be activated by a vibrational cleansing procedure involving items such as choming essences. These aid in the detoxification of your system and give your physical structure more vitality. As stated previously, any type of ailment can result from a blockage in the chakras. Vibrational purification results in the elimination of blockages and aids in system repair. However, it is essential to note that if your system has been damaged, it will not be easily repaired.

Smudging with white sage is another method for energizing the chakras. This method assists in purifying your body of negative energy. To accomplish this, you must burn white sage in a closed room so that the smoke from the burning sage permeates the space. Supposedly, this practice also helps remove negative energy from your home.

A third method for energizing your chakras is to have an expert perform a technique known as auric stroking on your chakra points. Professionals typically use special gems or stones for this purpose, as they believe that certain gems have the ability to heal the body on a spiritual level. Nevertheless, care must be taken when selecting the gem or stone, as only certain varieties of stones can be beneficial. Choosing the incorrect gem can cause damage to the chakras, which can exacerbate the blockage of your energy pathways.

Concentrate on your diet and choose a wholesome one as the fourth method. Additionally, drinking plenty of water is beneficial. Getting enough sleep and resting soundly at night are also beneficial. Sleep prevents stress, and relieving tension results in the opening of the body's energy channels.

The fifth method is to take in sufficient oxygen. Deep breathing provides the body with vitality and aids in overcoming blockages.

The sixth method for energizing chakras is to take an interest in nature and interact with your surroundings. The variety of colors in nature aid in the restoration of the soul. There are colors that aid in providing energy to the body or opening energy channels. These hues vary from individual to individual. This is because distinct colors produce different vibrations in various individuals. It is believed that the color green has healing properties and is beneficial to the spirit. This is why walking outside and observing nature aids in soul healing and makes you feel better. A beneficial practice is to go for a walk, take deep breaths, and imagine that you are inhaling the surrounding hues. This contributes significantly to the sensation of vigor.

Using specific categories of music or sounds is another method for awakening chakras. Sound has the ability to induce vibrations within the body and can assist in opening energy channels.

The eighth method of activating chakras is to stimulate your intellect. This contributes to increasing cerebral activity, which is essential for a healthy body. If your brain is healthy, you will be able to use your consciousness to control your chakras. It facilitates the activation of your chakras and the removal of any blockages. The fact that one of your chakras resides in the brain is another reason to concentrate on the brain. It is also the chakra with the maximum level. Therefore, increasing brain activity improves a person's overall chakra system and vitality level.

In addition, meditation is very effective at bringing calm to the inner self. It facilitates the removal of negative energy from the body and communication with the inner power zone. Meditation enables you to separate yourself from the outside world and focus solely on your inner requirements. This means that you prioritize your spiritual requirements over your physical needs. Therefore, it assists you in finding inner peace and connecting your mind and spirit. When you are tranquil, this results in the activation of your chakras.

The next rule is to believe in yourself, be content with what you receive, and adore your authentic self. This brings serenity to your mind and body and facilitates your soul connection. When a person begins to love himself, his earthly and transitory desires begin to fade away. It assists him in concentrating on his essence and immortal form, which leads to the activation of energy channels. Additionally, one must appreciate those around them. This reduces negative emotions of jealousy and contributes to soul harmony. It is a well-established scientific fact that when a person becomes enraged, his body generates toxic chemicals that result in negative energy. Conversely, when a person smiles or adores someone, his body provides him with positive energy.

It is essential to recognize that if a person cannot regulate his emotions, he cannot control his energy. It is essential to own your emotions and have the courage to express them. When emotions are suppressed, they tend to intensify and become a constant nuisance. This results in an uneasy feeling that prevents restful slumber, disrupts the sleep cycle, and expends a great deal of energy. Consequently, there is a blockage of the energy channels and chakras. Emotions have a close relationship with chakras, and when they are repressed, they harm the chakras and the psyche. To achieve mental and spiritual harmony, it is preferable to express oneself. For instance, if a person harbors resentment toward another for an extended period of time but does not express his anger to him or inform him that his habit is bothering him, he will waste a great deal of time and energy on negative thoughts about the other person. In the end, this will harm his chakras.

In addition to this, a person's energy channels are not obstructed if he possesses a sense of creativity. Creativity sharpens the mind and promotes harmony between the psyche and body. It causes the chakras to function more effectively. It is essential to remember that creativity can be demonstrated in anything that interests you and gives you the itch to explore.

Acting morally and ethically is a great method to protect your energy channel from obstruction. When a person engages in unethical behavior, such as scamming, lying, and deception, his energy channels are diverted to the negative side. It disrupts the equilibrium between his psyche and body, ultimately blocking his energy pathways. A person's energy system is primarily dependent on his efforts to act with the utmost integrity.

www.ingramcontent.com/pod-product-compliance
Lightning Source LLC
Chambersburg PA
CBHW050232120526
44590CB00016B/2048